They lived like this in
ANCIENT ROME

Author: **MARIE NEURATH**

Artist: **JOHN ELLIS**

of the Isotype Institute

A MAX PARRISH BOOK

MACDONALD EDUCATIONAL
London

© 1968 Isotype Institute Limited

Published by Macdonald and Co (Publishers) Ltd

49 Poland Street, London W.1

Printed by offset in Great Britain by

William Clowes & Sons, Limited, London, Beccles and Colchester

Reprinted 1971

SBN 356 00137 7

At the time of Julius Caesar, in the last century before Christ, poets and historians were writing about the beginning of Rome 700 years earlier. Some of them told that the founder and first king, Romulus, a son of their war-god Mars, was cast out as a baby with his twin brother and nursed by a she-wolf.

This picture might be of young Romulus, though it was found not in Rome but further north. It may have been made by the Etruscans who ruled the land and were Rome's masters for its first 250 years. They had skilled craftsmen when the Romans were nothing but simple peasants. The Etruscans made pictures in stone and brass, and painted on the walls of large underground tombs. They could write in an alphabet which was derived from the Greek, but their language cannot be translated today.

What we know about the early Etruscans comes mainly from the things they left behind. They brought the chariot and the horse with them when they arrived. When and from where they came, whether by land or by sea, is not known. But they must have come from a place where skills and knowledge were more advanced than in Italy.

Here an Etruscan in armour can be seen on horseback, fighting with a naked man, a Gaul. The Celtic Gauls had entered Italy from the north. They tried in vain to conquer the land of the Etruscans. They had spread into the northern plain of Italy.

The Etruscans were hunters and fishermen, farmers and merchants. Their rule had spread in Italy. They built several strong towns whose thick walls and arched gateways can be seen to the present day.

They knew about the smelting of iron and they mined iron ore. For their work they had many tools. They also made vases, but appreciated the Greeks' better products, which they imported. They were great traders. Some of their iron and other goods were taken to a market just beyond the river Tiber, where an island made the crossing easier. The area was marshy, and they built an arched underground canal to lead the water away. This market place was later to become the Forum of Rome, the city centre for commerce and trade, courts of law, temples and government assemblies.

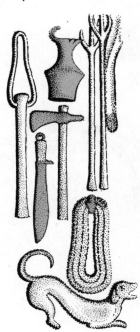

The Etruscans built large underground tombs outside their city walls.
These tombs can still be entered today. There one can see stone coffins
surrounded by pictures of Etruscan life. This wall painting shows a man
aiming at a flying sea bird with his sling. Below him are the waves
of the sea and four men in a fishing boat.

Other pictures show men at banquets and in religious ceremonies,
or strange animals and fabulous winged creatures.

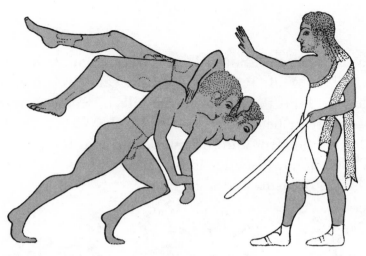

Here two men are seen wrestling. Another man with a stick is watching them. He may be a trainer or a judge in a contest.

Below is a scene of dance and music. The lyre, made of a tortoise shell and two horns, is like the old lyre which the Cretans and Greeks used.

Further south, in Sicily and South Italy, Greek colonists had arrived to found new cities. While they and the Etruscans lived their city life the people who built their huts on the hills of Rome were simple peasants who had their fields in the plains by the Tiber. As the land was poor and often flooded, and mosquitoes bred in the puddles, the peasants may have found it better to live in the hills. The first Rome was a group of farms and villages.

But even when Rome had become a large, independent city the Romans sacrificed bulls, sheep, pigs and the fruits of the field to the gods, as their peasant forefathers had done. Every action of their daily life was ruled and furthered by one of their many gods, and each had to get his due. Each family was ruled absolutely by the father, and the laws of the family were more and more extended to cover a wider community.

In the beginning each family on its farm did everything for its own food, shelter, and clothing. But later, by the time of Julius Caesar, in a more urban way of life, milling and baking were done in big establishments on a larger scale. Much of the wheat was imported.

 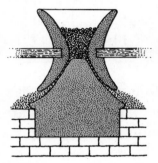

Many millstones like this one were worked side by side. Donkeys were harnessed to the poles and pulled the upper stone round and round. The grains poured into the open top were ground to flour between the turning and the fixed cone-shaped stones. The flour fell on the rim. The picture below shows a bakery. A group of men are kneading the dough, another man is loading the oven, and at the end the distribution is shown: a man with a writing tablet watches, the bread is weighed on a big balance and handed to the waiting men. Many people in Caesar's Rome received bread free of charge. This giving played an important part in the politics of Rome, and it was continued by the emperors.

Cleaning and dyeing clothes also became a commercial business in the town. These pictures are from a house in which the finishing processes of clothmaking took place during Caesar's lifetime. The first pictures show fullers at work: the woven material is steeped in water and beaten with feet and hands. The next picture shows a man "carding": with a hard brush or thistle the cloth is given a looser and softer surface. Another man carries a basket-like structure on which the cloth is spread for drying.

Finally the material was put under a linen press like this. Similar presses were in use to press oil from olives.

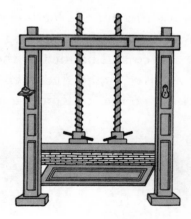

In early times the Romans made clothing mostly of wool from their sheep, and every girl had to learn to spin and weave.

Around the market places in the towns there were many shops for the various goods for sale. Here a piece of cloth is shown to the customers. It is large enough to be used as a toga, a garment which the men wore over their tunics as a coat.

This shop has scarves and cushions on show, and the customers are women.

Not only the cushions, but also the wicker chair look as if they might be in use today. Comfortable chairs like this can be seen in many of the pictures that the Romans carved in stone.

Here we see blacksmiths at work, forging iron and steel.

Knives and sickles of many shapes were on sale in the shops. Some were very sharp and were used as razors. The fashion of shaving off the beard began to spread during the early Empire.

Locksmiths invented safer locks and made complicated keys. Until Augustus' time there were no police for the difficult task of keeping order in the narrow winding streets of Rome. These were lined with tenement houses several stories high which became more and more overcrowded.

There was no street lighting. Whoever had to
go out into the rather dangerous streets at
night preferred to take a torchbearer with him.

In the house, candles were used.
This little torchbearer figure
is a candle holder.

Oil lamps, made of stone, clay
or bronze, were also used.
Through the central opening, olive
oil was poured in. A wick was
put in the oil so that its end
stuck out of the smaller hole
where a flame was lit. Care had
to be taken that the wick was
readjusted as it burned away.

Though they were dark, the streets were noisy at night in the city of
Rome. During daytime the narrow streets were thronged with people,
and Julius Caesar forbade wheeled transport. Only at night could the
cartloads of food and goods for Rome's million people be brought in.

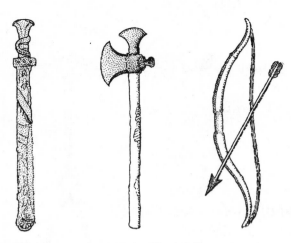

In early times every Roman citizen had to give military service and be skilled in the use of sword, axe and bow. Rome was a military power.

But every soldier of old Rome was also a peasant, and wherever he went as conqueror he also took his plough.

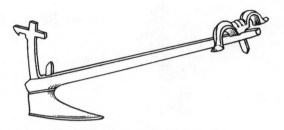

The new farmland and the people on it had to be within easy reach. Therefore the Romans needed good roads, and the soldiers themselves were the road builders. The practice of road building, started in Rome's neighbourhood, continued in the ever growing empire.

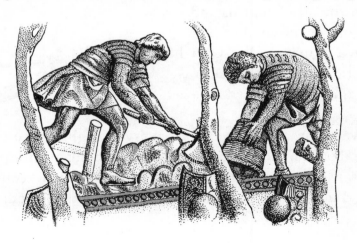

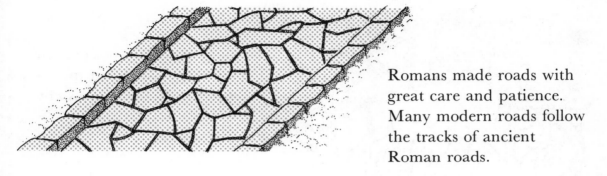

Romans made roads with great care and patience. Many modern roads follow the tracks of ancient Roman roads.

In squares the stones were often laid in pleasant patterns.

In private houses and public baths skilled workers designed the famous mosaic floors with smaller stones of various colours.

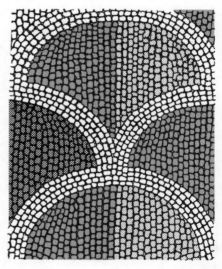

Sometimes mosaics decorated walls. Pictures of animals and plants, even portraits of people, were made in this way.

The roads were used not only by
the marching legions and the
messengers to Rome, but also by
private travellers in coaches
or on horseback.

Coach travel might have been even quicker had the Romans known better
about the harnessing of horses. The collar pressed against the throats
of the horses, who could hardly breathe when they pulled the carts.

This picture shows the base of the
golden milestone in the Forum of
Rome, the centre of the system of
roads throughout the empire.

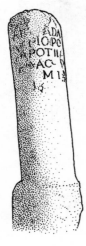

Everywhere milestones marked the roads and
gave places and distances in the beautiful
lettering which the Romans carved into the
stone. Travel in Roman times was quicker
and safer than ever before and for many
centuries after.

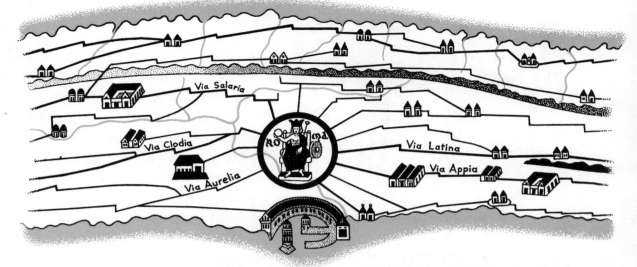

The saying "All roads lead to Rome" was true for many centuries. At the time when the Roman Empire had grown to its greatest extent a designer made a map of all the main roads. This was found in a library in the Middle Ages. The map is drawn in such a way that road distances are shown, but the shapes of the country are very distorted. Here is a small part of the map, around the city of Rome. The names of some of the famous roads are still in use today. Along the Via Appia there are many grave monuments of ancient times.

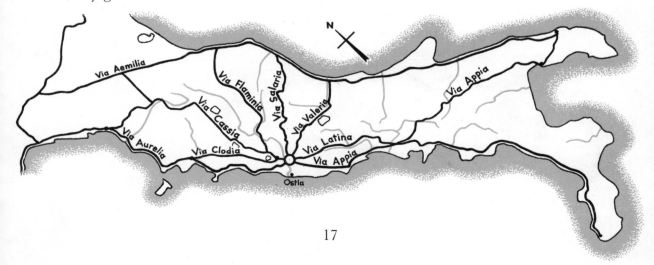

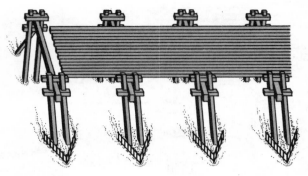

Every army had to cross rivers. Caesar himself described in one of his books how his soldiers constructed a wooden bridge across the river Rhine. This drawing was made from his description.

The pillars of another military bridge were made of stone and have survived to the present day. The wooden superstructure was made of shorter timbers arranged in arches.

Such wooden construction was also needed in preparation for the arches of stone as in the bridge below. Among the oldest Roman stone bridges which crossed the Tiber were the two which connected the Tiber island with both shores.

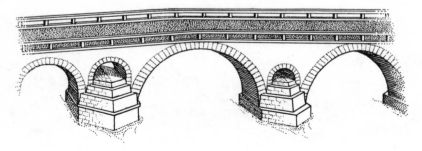

Special religious ceremonies took place when bridges were built. The priestly office of "pontifex maximus" – chief bridge builder – was one of the greatest honours a Roman citizen could achieve, and Julius Caesar himself held this title. It has continued in use to the present day as one of the titles given to the Pope in Rome. The quickest way for the armies to cross rivers was to put boats side by side to carry a series of planks on which the soldiers could walk across.

Simple rowing boats were also used for river transport. These two pictures show barrels being loaded and transported by ship.

The Roman landsmen took to the sea rather late, forced by seafaring people with whom the Romans came into conflict. There was little aggression from Etruscan sailors, but much more from the Phoenician people in Carthage on the African coast opposite Sicily, where the Phoenicians also ruled until the Romans captured the island.

When the Romans had to fight the Phoenicians they needed harbours and lighthouses.

They also had to have warships from which their soldiers could fight. Rome achieved all this. It preserved its independence from the powerful attackers and through its victories became ruler of the whole of Italy, including the Etruscans and the Greek colonies in the south. It razed Carthage to the ground and soon afterwards ruled over the whole Western Mediterranean.

Rome did not destroy the Greek way of life, but absorbed much of it.
At the time of Caesar, groups of villas like these on seaward slopes
belonged to wealthy Romans. They built in the Greek style for living
in the southern sun. Boats were now used for pleasure; houses and
gardens allowed the enjoyment of nature. Buildings and sculpture
added to the beauty of the scenery.

Towns of a different type, with a regular grid of streets, four
gates and a central square, were founded throughout the empire. They
developed out of military camps. This origin can still be traced in
many towns of Europe, North Africa and the Near East today.

There was a great change in the Roman way of life after Rome became the centre of an empire. Many Roman farmers and soldiers grew rich and had servants and slaves.

With more leisure, home life became more varied in enjoyment. Works of art, with which the early hardworking Romans could not be bothered, became a part of life.

The vase shown here was made by Greeks living in Italy, south of Rome. Their work was now highly appreciated and, like Etruscan art, was being collected.

The scenes represented in vase paintings were understood, and Greek gods were added to the Roman and given new names. Zeus became Jupiter, Ares became Mars. March, the first month in Caesar's new calendar, was named after Mars, the father of Romulus.

From the Greeks the Romans learned the use of coins. Their earliest "money" had been cattle; their wealth was counted in heads of cattle. Their first metal "money" was heavy bits of bronze showing the shape of a bull, as pictured on the top of the next page.

This early Roman coin shows the Roman sign for 10, X; its unit is called "denarius" – the origin of the English "d" for penny in £ s d. The two riders carrying a star, Castor and Pollux, had a temple in Rome. In very early times they were believed to have saved the Romans in a desperate battle.

Caesar's coin with Venus on one side shows the Trojan Aeneas carrying his father – a son of Venus – on their flight from captured Troy. Aeneas was said to have settled in Italy and Caesar claimed him as an ancestor.

The last coin commemorates the end of Caesar. On one side is the head of Brutus who led Caesar's opponents. On the other, the cap of liberty and the swords with which Caesar was killed.

PΩMAIΩN   ROMANO

Some early Roman coins still show writing in the alphabet used by the Greeks. Later the Romans changed the lettering to their own.

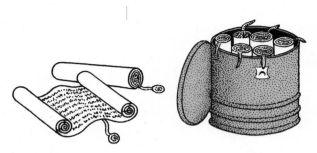

Sometimes the rich Romans had Greek scholars as slaves to teach their children. Greek became a second language of the educated, who read the Greek books and went to Athens to study.

Books were in the shape of long strips of paper or parchment, one side of which was covered with writing. They were kept rolled up. A little tag which was attached to them carried the title.

In a private library such rolls were kept in drums with decorated lids. In a larger library they were stacked on shelves.

Elementary teaching was restricted to reading, writing and arithmetic, and teachers did little to whet an appetite for knowledge. But the tutors of the upper-class boys covered a wider field. They gave a lead into the study of Greek writings in all fields – history, science, philosophy, religion and literature.

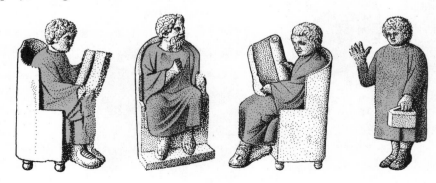

Great care was taken to develop precise use of the language and public speaking. These skills were essential in Roman public life. Lawyers pleaded in the courts, generals addressed their armies, senators, dictators and emperors addressed the people in the Forum. There was a raised platform, the rostrum, from which the leaders spoke to the people standing below.

After speech and debate in the Roman Senate, laws were made for the whole Republic. The heads of the old Roman families had agreed among themselves how they should regulate their life together. When more people joined them they found ways to adapt their rules so that a wider community could be formed. When the Greeks' general ideas about law and order were added, the scope became even wider and claimed to be worldwide. On the other hand, nobody but the citizens present in Rome could partake in government. The Romans, who thought out and established laws which were the basis of modern laws, did not think of the possibility that the citizens in the provinces could elect and send a man to Rome to represent them in government. After the Republic, the Emperor ruled and the Senate became of little importance.

Rome was the hub of the world.
At the time of Caesar its population
grew rapidly. Here free bread was
distributed and games and shows
kept the masses contented.
Many pictures show what new forms
the old sports took in the Rome
of the Caesars.

Strong men, mostly chosen from prisoners of war or condemned criminals,
were exhibited struggling with wild beasts.

Others were fighting with each other
as gladiators. The Roman public got
used to the spectacle of seeing men
killed. They took a passionate interest
in this brutal slaughter, and some men
volunteered to fight.

For these shows, great arenas were built in every Roman city throughout the Empire. The largest of all were those for chariot racing – the circuses. They were not circular like our circuses, but elongated with a low decorated wall along the centre spine, around which the race took place.

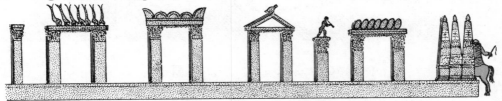

Rome's largest circus had three cone-shaped pillars at the turning point.

The round arenas for sport and shows were called amphitheatres. They had rows of seats, built like steps, all around. In the theatres the seats took up only about three-quarters of the circle. The rest was taken up by the stage on which the actors performed. Under the open sky the voices of the actors could be heard by the large audience. The actors wore masks with big openings for the mouth.

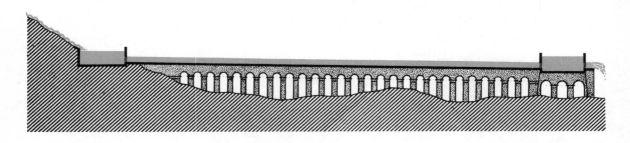

No town in the world was so well served with water as Rome. From springs in the wooded mountains water was carried to Rome over the plains, in long stone gulleys which were supported by hundreds of arches. From large tanks in the town the water was distributed to private houses, the huge public baths which served as social recreation centres, and the many fountains in squares and gardens.

Rome has remained famous for its fountains ever since. Smaller towns imitated the practice. This picture was painted on the wall of a house in Pompeii at the foot of Mount Vesuvius.

Another picture there shows
a villa as it might have been
built against the steep slope
of a hill, with steps and
balconies, open or roofed
terraces, sunshades and
flowering gardens.

Waste water was also taken away, in ways already devised by the
Etruscans, and bathing and sanitation were well developed.

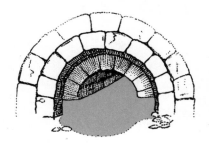

New equipment was invented
for pumping and plumbing.
Much of it was forgotten
by the people in the Middle
Ages and had to be invented
again in modern times.

The Romans usually tried to link the new with the old. From early times, religion was closely connected with daily life, and the Romans did not hesitate to adopt new gods to join theirs when new practices became part of their life. But they also continued their old worship of Lar, the household god. He is shown here with horn and bowl as giver of all good things.

Like everything else, grapes were the gift of a god. Harvesting them and pressing the juice out of them with dancing feet to the sound of music was performed like a ritual.

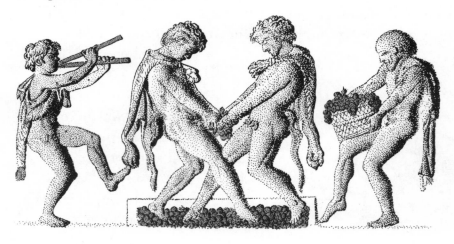

When Greek gods became known, it was Dionysos with his new Latin name of Bacchus who was the god of wine to whom sacrifice was made.

Ever more gods were added when the Romans conquered new people. Many soldiers worshipped Mithras, a god from the east. Mithras temples were built throughout the Empire.

The Egyptian goddess Isis with Serapis, the chief Egyptian god, was also worshipped in Rome under the emperors. This picture shows priests and priestesses in Egyptian worship.

On one of the oldest Roman coins the head of their god Janus with its two faces is shown. He was a watchful god, looking to all sides. His temple was always open when Rome was at war, so that he could keep his eyes on Rome's good fortune.

When peace followed war the temple was closed. It was one of the great achievements of the Roman Empire after Caesar that imperial peace remained practically undisturbed for two hundred years.